NATURAL WONDERS

Mauna Loa

The Largest Volcano in the United States

Christine Webster

WEIGL PUBLISHERS INC.

Published by Weigl Publishers Inc.
350 5th Avenue, Suite 3304
New York, NY 10118-0069
USA

Web site: www.weigl.com

Library of Congress Cataloging-in-Publication Data

Webster, Christine.
  The Mauna Loa / Christine Webster.
    v. cm. -- (Natural wonders of the USA)
Includes bibliographical references and index.
Contents: A massive wonder -- Where in the world -- A trip back in time -- A lesson in plate tectonics -- Life on Mauna Loa -- Early explorers -- The big picture -- The people of Mauna Loa -- A heritage inspired by Mauna Loa -- Must see and do -- Key issues: relocation? -- Time lines -- What have you learned?
  ISBN 1-59036-040-0 (lib. bound : alk. paper) – ISBN 1-59036-162-8 (pbk.)
  1. Mauna Loa (Hawaii Island, Hawaii)--Juvenile literature. [1. Mauna Loa (Hawaii Island, Hawaii) 2. Volcanoes.] I. Title. II. Series.
  DU629.M34 W43 2002
  996.9'1--dc21
                                    2002013609
Printed in the United States of America
1 2 3 4 5 6 7 8 9 0 07 06 05 04 03

Project Coordinators
Michael Lowry
Tina Schwartzenberger

Copy Editor
Frances Purslow

Design
Terry Paulhus

Layout
Virginia Boulay

Photo Researchers
Nicole Bezic King
Wendy Cosh

Contents

A Massive Wonder

Mauna Loa, the largest volcano on Earth, rises more than 13,000 feet above the Pacific Ocean. Mauna Loa is so large that it covers half the island of Hawai'i.

Mauna Loa is a shield volcano. This type of volcano has gently-sloped sides that look like a warrior's shield. The gradual rise in height is the result of more than 150 separate eruptions.

People have been living near Mauna Loa for thousands of years. Despite predicted eruptions, they continue to do so. Visitors and those living near Mauna Loa may witness a hot **lava** flow up close.

Visitors to Mauna Loa can hike to the top to see the fascinating scenery.

Mauna Loa Facts:

- Mauna Loa is approximately 60 miles long and 30 miles wide.

- Mauna Loa covers 2,035 square miles.

- When measured from the sea floor, Mauna Loa is 56,000 feet high—taller than Mount Everest.

- In 1984, Mauna Loa erupted and covered 11,800 acres with lava. The lava created 180 acres of new land offshore.

- The name *Mauna Loa* means "long mountain."

- Eruptions have lasted between 1 and 1,200 days.

- Mauna Loa has erupted thirty-nine times since 1832.

- Mauna Loa first erupted more than 700,000 years ago.

- On August 1, 1916, Mauna Loa became part of Hawai'i Volcanoes National Park.

Mauna Loa Locator

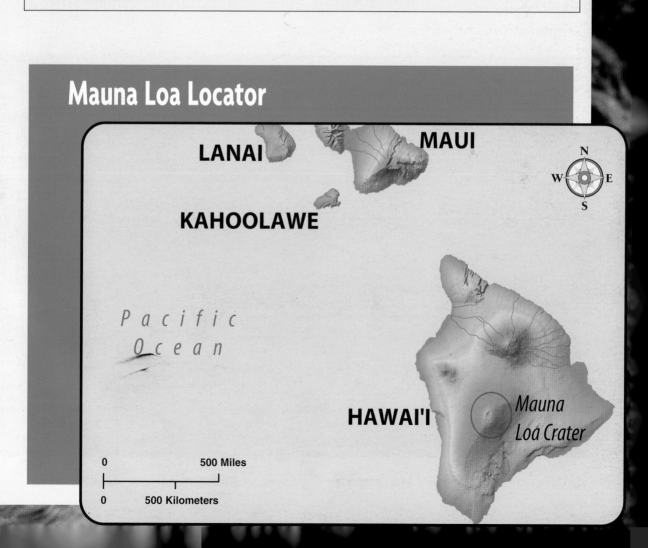

LANAI

MAUI

KAHOOLAWE

N
W E
S

Pacific
Ocean

HAWAI'I

Mauna Loa Crater

0   500 Miles

0   500 Kilometers

Where in the World?

Mauna Loa is located on the island of Hawai'i. The state of Hawai'i is the fourth-smallest state in the United States. It consists of eight main volcanic islands, which form a chain in the Pacific Ocean. These islands are visible parts of a much larger undersea mountain range. The range is 1,600 miles long and is called the Hawai'ian Chain.

Mauna Loa has a varied tropical climate. Near the coast, the climate is humid, yet the winters are dry. Rainfall is heaviest on the northeastern slopes of Mauna Loa. At low elevations, the average temperature is between 72° and 79° Fahrenheit. Temperatures are slightly lower in the winter. Snow can cover the summit of Mauna Loa in the winter. Winter can also bring **cyclonic** storms and heavy rains.

■ **During heavy winter storms, 3 to 4 inches of rain can fall on Hawai'i in 1 hour.**

Eruptions

Mauna Loa is an active volcano. This means that it erupts often and is expected to continue erupting. Some past eruptions have covered areas the size of 100 football fields with lava. Other eruptions have destroyed villages and towns. Most of Mauna Loa's eruptions were predicted, so residents had time to safely leave their homes.

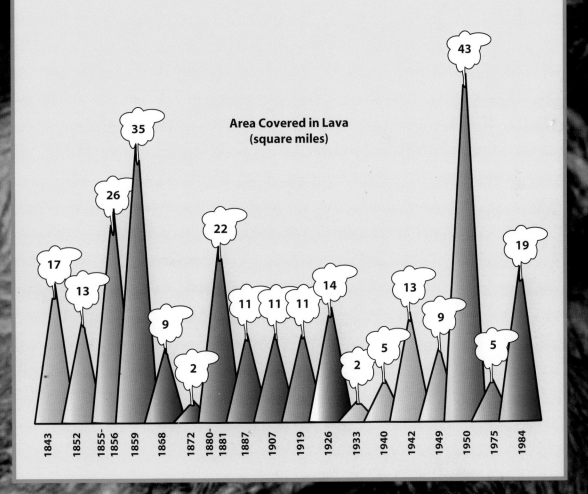

Area Covered in Lava (square miles)

Year	Area
1843	17
1852	13
1855-1856	26
1859	35
1868	9
1872	2
1880-1881	11
1887	11
1907	11
1919	14
1926	22
1933	2
1940	5
1942	13
1949	9
1950	43
1975	5
1984	19

A Trip Back in Time

housands of years ago, small cracks appeared in the floor of the Pacific Ocean. Hot lava seeped out, forming mounds on the sea floor. This process of lava seeping and hardening was repeated many times. Mauna Loa grew each time a new layer of lava was added on top of old, hardened lava. Eventually, the volcano rose above the water and became an island.

The people of Hawai'i named Mauna Loa's peak *Moku'aweoweo*. Moku'aweoweo is a type of crater called a **caldera**. *Moku* is the word for a section of coastal land or an islet. *Aweoweo* is a type of red Hawai'ian fish. The red fish is believed to represent the lava.

Mauna Loa is believed to be about 700,000 years old.

Types of Lava

Volcanoes produce two types of lava. They are called *pahoehoe* and *a'a*. Scientists throughout the world use these Hawai'ian words to describe lava.

Pahoehoe

Pahoehoe is smooth, thin, runny lava. This type of lava occurs during eruptions with high temperatures. When pahoehoe cools, it forms a smooth rope-like surface. It can even form into tubes under the crust. These lava tubes are sometimes large enough to walk through.

A'a

A'a lava is rough and sharp as a knife. When flowing, a'a moves in surges. When it dries, it forms jagged boulders. If you tried walking or climbing on this lava, you would likely be cut.

A Lesson in Plate Tectonics

Scientists believe that Earth's crust is divided into sections called plates. The plates move slowly, about 1 inch per year. Some plates come together and collide, which causes earthquakes. Other plates move apart and form volcanoes. This belief is known as plate tectonics.

Deep in Earth's core, the temperature is so hot that it melts rocks. When the rocks melt, they expand and move. This liquid rock mixes with gases, forming magma. Rising magma hits Earth's surface. Pressure builds, and eventually, Earth's crust cracks. This is known as an eruption. When magma seeps through the cracks, it is called lava. The hole that magma escapes from is called a volcano.

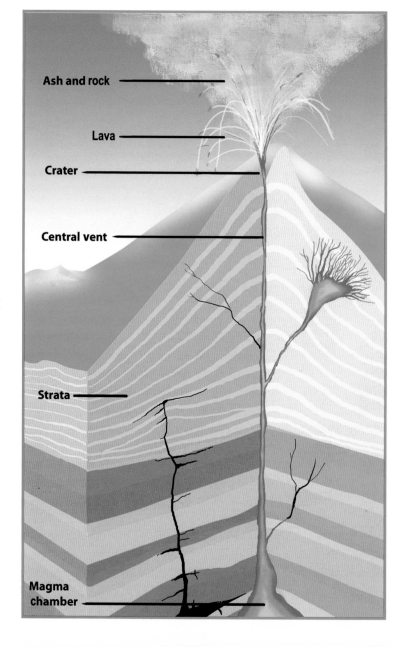

Ash and rock

Lava

Crater

Central vent

Strata

Magma chamber

■ **Hot magma rises through volcanoes and erupts in the form of lava.**

Birth of an Island

The Hawai'ian Islands were formed over a hot spot in the middle of the Pacific plate. As the Pacific plate moves northwest, it carries with it new, hardened lava, volcanoes, and islands. A new volcano is then formed over the hot spot. The new volcano does not move. As new volcanoes are formed, they are also carried away from the hot spot, creating a chain of islands. This is how the Hawai'ian Chain was formed. Today, the Hawai'ian Chain consists of eight main islands—Hawai'i, Kahoolawe, Kauai, Lanai, Maui, Molokai, Niihau, and Oahu.

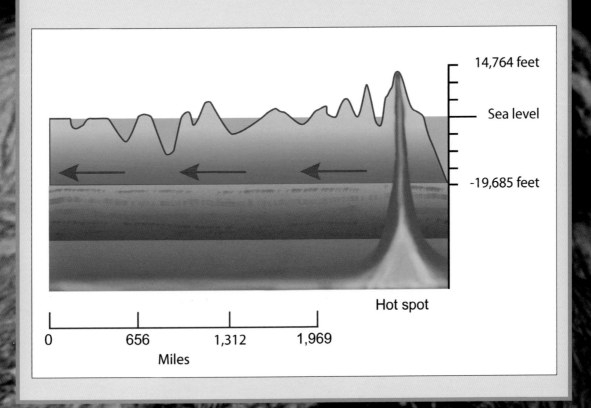

Life on Mauna Loa

Hawai'i has a variety of native and introduced plants and animals. Hawai'i's native plants evolved from those carried to Hawai'i by wind, water, and on the wings of birds. Ships brought animals to Hawai'i.

Mauna Loa is divided into ten vegetation zones. Each zone is home to different kinds of plants and animals. The upper slopes are dry and barren. At lower **altitudes**, plant life includes silversword, *napuu* trees, and *mamane*. Hawai'ian geese and hoary bats can also be found at lower altitudes.

Fern forests are the first vegetation to grow on new lava flows. They thrive in high-altitude rain forests. The lower coastal areas have mesquite and cactus. A common sight on Mauna Loa is the state tree, the *kukui*.

In 1962, sixty-seven kalij pheasants were brought to Hawai'i from game farms in Michigan and Texas.

Puzzler

When lava erupts from volcanoes, it permanently changes the surrounding landscape.

Q How has the changing landscape of Mauna Loa affected plants and animals?

A Hawai'i's changing landscape has caused many plants and animals to become **endangered** or **extinct**. This is because each new lava flow from Mauna Loa creates isolated habitats. Species must also adjust to changes in temperature and rainfall.

Early Explorers

The first people to see Mauna Loa were Polynesians. They arrived between AD 600 and 1200. Today, some Polynesians are called Hawai'ians. In 1779, Captain James Cook became the first European to explore the island. The Hawai'ians treated Cook to a celebration with ceremonies, feasts, and games. Later, after a disagreement, the Hawai'ians stole Cook's boat. In return, Cook took their chief hostage. A fight broke out, and one of the Hawai'ians struck Cook, killing him.

In 1794, Archibald Menzies became the first European to climb Mauna Loa. On June 20, 1832, Menzies recorded the first known eruption of Mauna Loa. The eruption lasted twenty-one days.

About thirty years later, in 1859, Mauna Loa erupted again. It destroyed two coastal villages at Wainanali'i and Kiholo. At the time, it was the longest eruption in the state, lasting 300 days. It was at this eruption that observers first identified how a'a lava formed.

■ **Captain James Cook is best known for the careful, detailed way he documented his discoveries.**

Biography

Thomas Augustus Jaggar (1871–1953)

Thomas Augustus Jaggar was raised in Philadelphia, Pennsylvania. He studied **geology** at Harvard University. In 1902, he began studying volcano disasters. These experiences led him to a career in **volcanology**. Jaggar believed there was a need to study volcanoes before they erupted. He felt that this research could save lives. In 1912, Jaggar helped create the Hawai'ian Volcano Observatory. Today, Hawai'ian volcanoes are constantly monitored, and most eruptions are predicted. The studies at the Hawai'ian Volcano Observatory have helped save numerous lives.

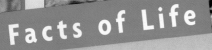

Facts of Life

Born: 1871

Hometown: Philadelphia, Pennsylvania

Occupation: geologist, volcanologist, teacher

Died: 1953

The Big Picture

More than half of the world's volcanoes above sea level are found along the edge of the Pacific plate in the "Ring of Fire." The Ring of Fire is an arc that stretches from New Zealand, along the eastern edge of Asia, north across Alaska's Aleutian Islands, and south along the coasts of North America and South America. Most of the volcanoes are still underwater. The Ring of Fire is known for its frequent earthquakes and volcanic eruptions. Some of the most well-known volcanoes are found in the Ring of Fire. These famous volcanoes include Mount St. Helens in the United States, Mount Fuji in Japan, Mount Pinatubo in the Philippines, and Popocatépetl in Mexico.

Map Legend

	Volcano	Country	Elevation (ft)	Last Eruption
1.	Mount Hudson	Chile	6,250	1991
2.	Cotopaxi	Ecuador	19,388	1904
3.	El Chichon	Mexico	3,478	1982
4.	Popocatépetl	Mexico	17,880	1920–1922
5.	Paricutin	Mexico	10,400	1943–1952
6.	Mount St. Helens	Washington, U.S.	8,364	1980
7.	Augustine Volcano	Alaska, U.S.	4,200	1986
8.	Mount Fuji	Japan	12,388	1707
9.	Mount Pinatubo	Philippines	4,872	1991
10.	Mount Agung	Indonesia	10,308	1963
11.	Rabaul	Papua New Guinea	2,257	1994
12.	Mount Ruapehu	New Zealand	9,175	1995
13.	Mauna Loa	Hawai'i, U.S.	13,680	1984
14.	Kilauea	Hawai'i, U.S.	4,190	1983–2002

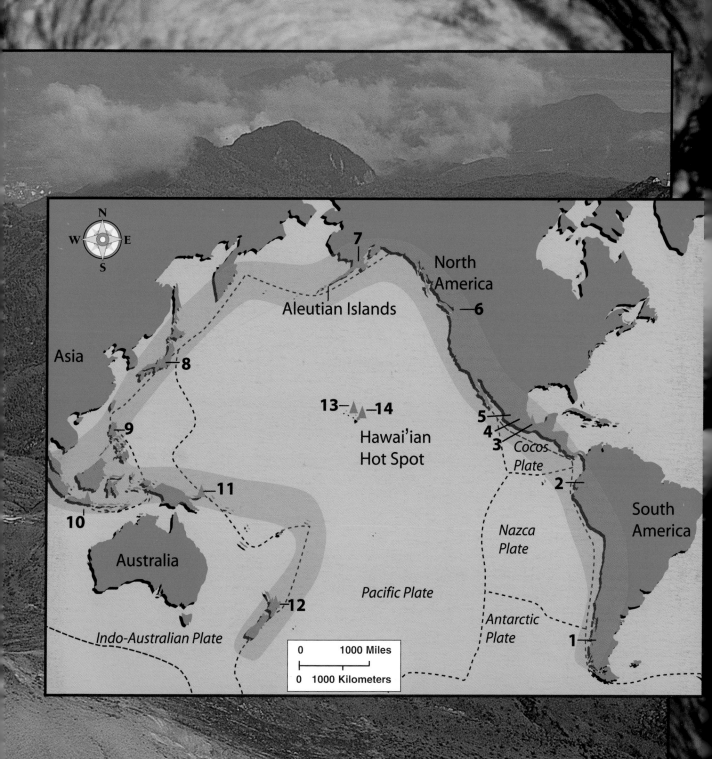

N W E S

7

North America

Aleutian Islands

6

Asia

8

13—▲▲—14

Hawai'ian Hot Spot

5
4
3 Cocos Plate

2

9

South America

11

Nazca Plate

10

Australia

Antarctic Plate

1

Pacific Plate

12

Indo-Australian Plate

| 0 | 1000 Miles |
| 0 | 1000 Kilometers |

The People of Mauna Loa

Thousands of years ago, Polynesians arrived in Hawai'i by canoe. These early settlers lived in villages along the coast or in valleys. They fished, farmed, and ate wild plants. Chiefs were the heads of the society. Priests and other professionals ranked below the chiefs. The commoners farmed and fished.

The Polynesians believed that gods were the forces of nature. As a result, they respected and worshiped the environment and did not fear the forces of nature. Despite the danger of lava flows, villages were built on Mauna Loa. Today, Hawai'ians continue to develop roads around volcano cones. They also build homes on the steep slopes.

▬ Capes and helmets of red and yellow feathers are worn in traditional Hawai'ian ceremonies.

Puzzler

Many people of Hawai'i do not fear volcanoes. Hawai'ians have worked and lived on the slopes of Mauna Loa for thousands of years. In fact, the villages of Pahala and Volcano can only be reached by hiking over lava flows.

Q How have indigenous peoples benefited from living on Mauna Loa?

A There are many benefits to living on Mauna Loa. Eruptions leave behind very fertile soils for farming. Electricity can be created using steam from the volcanoes. Tourists who visit the area create jobs in hotels, restaurants, and gift shops.

An Eruption of Art

Mauna Loa has inspired artists for thousands of years. Early Hawai'ians used natural items, such as rocks and shells, to portray the beauty of Mauna Loa. Mauna Loa is also the subject of stories, dances, and songs. Hulas are traditional dances that Hawai'ians use to tell stories without words.

In the 1880s, Howard Hitchcock and Jules Tavenier climbed to the top of Mauna Loa to paint on canvas. Today, local artists continue to climb the volcano. The stunning view provides inspiration for paintings and photographs.

Located next to the Visitor Center at the Hawai'i Volcanoes National Park is the Volcano Art Center. The center features artwork by local Hawai'ian artists.

The hula dance was originally a religious dance. Today, the dance tells a story.

Mauna Loa Folklore

Hawai'ians believe Pele, the Polynesian Fire Goddess of Hawai'i, lives in the craters of volcanoes. She is the lava that spews from the Hawai'ian volcanoes. She can disguise herself in many forms.

A story tells that once, two brothers were riding sleds down ramps on the southwestern coast of Mauna Loa. The ramps were lined with grass. A beautiful woman approached and challenged them to a race. The brothers soon realized that she was Pele. She was looking for a boyfriend. Scared, they ran away. Taking on the form of lava, Pele chased them. She caught the brothers at the coastline and turned them into matching hills known today as *Na Pu'u o Pele*, which means "hills of Pele."

Natural Attractions

If you visit Hawai'i, allow time to tour the Hawai'i Volcanoes National Park. It is the largest of Hawai'i's five parks. The park is home to Mauna Loa. Kilauea, the world's most active volcano, is also located here.

When visiting the park, take a few hours or even days to hike the park trails. Get a firsthand view of the natural history of Mauna Loa and Kilauea. You can backpack, bird-watch, or camp along the trails.

Visit the Thomas A. Jaggar Museum. It offers a glimpse into Hawai'ian culture. From the museum, you will have a magnificent view of Mauna Loa and Kilauea.

Take a drive on the 11-mile loop road. This road circles the summit of the Kilauea volcano. The drive will take you through a desert and a rain forest.

Be Prepared
In case of a possible eruption of Mauna Loa, visitors need to be prepared.
1. Prepare yourself by learning about volcanic eruptions.
2. Learn where the lava would flow, and determine the safest route out.
3. Be prepared, and have an emergency plan.
4. Know the safety zones in the area that have been selected for safe **evacuation**.

Safety First

Read the following tips for viewing lava safely. Understanding the hazards is important to your safety. Follow these rules and you will enjoy a safe and spectacular viewing of volcanic lava.

Do not stand or walk in or under volcanic fumes. These fumes contain high amounts of hydrochloric acid, sulfuric acid, and glass particles. The acids can make it difficult to breathe. Glass particles can harm eyes, causing temporary blindness.

Do not go near lava when it flows through vegetation. When lava covers plants, the lack of oxygen produces **methane gas**. If methane gas ignites, the ground explodes, throwing debris and rocks.

When lava enters the ocean, seawater boils and explodes. Rocks and lava blast up and are thrown hundreds of yards onto land. Stand 1,500 feet away from steam clouds.

When lava enters the ocean, new land, called a bench, forms. These benches can collapse without warning. Stay about 1,500 feet inland, away from "bench areas."

Relocation

During the last eruption of Mauna Loa in 1984, lava flowed within 4 miles of the city of Hilo. Hilo, which was built on an old lava flow, is home to 47,000 people. Other residents of Mauna Loa have not been so lucky. Past eruptions have destroyed entire villages, ruined crops, and damaged roads and structures.

■ **Lava from numerous volcanic eruptions covers sections of the Chain of Craters Road in Hawai'i Volcanoes National Park.**

Despite the dangers of living near a volcano, many people continue to do so. Some people believe that these people should be moved for their own safety. Read the following arguments and make your own decision about **relocation**.

Should the local population of Mauna Loa be relocated for their own safety?

YES	NO
The residents of Mauna Loa should be moved for their own safety.	With scientific technology, warnings are given in advance of eruptions. This can help save lives. Mauna Loa may not erupt for hundreds of years.
Relocating the residents will save money in the future. If the residents are moved, the government will not have to rebuild towns and replace people's lost possessions if lava destroys their homes.	The cost of relocating an entire town or city would be enormous and time consuming.
 By re-using the current supplies of a town to relocate citizens, the government would not have to use new resources to rebuild a village. This is better for the environment.	Relocating Hawai'ians is against their rights. Many Hawai'ians believe strongly in the natural environment and do not fear its forces. Relocating them against their will would ignore their beliefs and violate their right to make their own decisions.

Time Line

4.5 billion years ago
Earth's plates begin to separate, and volcanoes form on the sea floor.

6 million years ago
Kauai Island is formed.

3.4 million years ago
Oahu Island is formed.

2.5 million years ago
Waianae Island is formed.

1.8 million years ago
Maui Island is formed.

1 million years ago
Mauna Kea is formed.

0.7 million years ago
Mauna Loa surfaces, forming the island of Hawai'i.

200,000 years ago
The volcano Loihi is born.

AD 600–1200
Polynesians travel by canoe and arrive in Hawai'i.

It has taken more than 700,000 years for Mauna Loa to reach its current height.

The Captain James Cook Monument was built in 1878, near the site of his death. It stands on the shore of Kealakekua Bay.

1200
Another group of settlers arrive in Hawai'i from Tahiti.

1778
Captain James Cook explores the island.

1779
Captain James Cook settles on Hawai'i. He is killed later the same year.

1779
About 80,000 people live in Hawai'i.

Lava flow closed the Chain of Craters Road in 1986.

Missionaries banned public performances of the hula dance in the early 1800s. The ban lasted 50 years.

1868
Mauna Loa erupts and causes the largest earthquake in Hawai'ian history.

1916
The United States makes Mauna Loa part of the Hawai'i Volcanoes National Park. It is the thirteenth national park in the United States.

1926
Mauna Loa erupts, resulting in many earthquakes and the destruction of the village of Ho'öpüloa.

1950
Mauna Loa erupts and buries many villages. This is the largest eruption on record.

1984
Mauna Loa's most recent eruption covers 11,800 acres of surrounding hills with lava. The eruption lasts 3 weeks.

1794
Archibald Menzies becomes the first non-Hawai'ian to climb Mauna Loa.

1820
A group of Christian missionaries arrive in Hawai'i from the United States.

1832
Archibald Menzies records the first known eruption of Mauna Loa.

1859
Mauna Loa erupts and destroys the coastal town of Wainanali'i.

2002
Mauna Loa shows increased activity.

What Have You Learned?

True or False?

Decide whether the following statements are true or false. If the statement is false, make it true.

1. The State of Hawai'i consists of eight major volcanic islands called the Hawai'ian Chain.

2. It is safe to stand on a bench or newly hardened lava.

3. Magma is called lava when it breaks through Earth's crust.

4. The largest eruption of Mauna Loa on record occurred in 1950.

5. Nobody lives near Mauna Loa because of eruptions.

ANSWERS

1. True
2. False. It is never safe to stand on benches. They could collapse into the sea.
3. True
4. True
5. False. Many people live in villages along the slopes of Mauna Loa.

Short Answer

Answer the following questions using information from the book.

1. What type of volcano is Mauna Loa?

2. How did animal life get to Hawai'i?

3. Mauna Loa produces two types of lava. One type is called a'a. Name the other.

4. What is the theory that scientists use to explain the movement of Earth's plates?

5. To survive Mauna Loa's changing geology, what must local plants and animals do?

6. Name the material that spews out of volcanoes.

ANSWERS
1. A shield volcano
2. By ship
3. Pahoehoe
4. Plate tectonics
5. Adapt
6. Lava

Multiple Choice

Choose the best answer in the following questions.

1. What does *Mauna Loa* mean?
   a) "fat mountain"
   b) "long mountain"
   c) "tall mountain"
   d) "big mountain"

2. A shield volcano is a volcano that is:
   a) gently sloped
   b) steep
   c) cone-shaped
   d) none of the above

3. Hawai'ians were originally from:
   a) Polynesia
   b) China
   c) Europe
   d) North America

4. The first recorded eruption of Mauna Loa was in:
   a) 1912
   b) 1984
   c) 1832
   d) 1780

ANSWERS
1. b
2. a
3. a
4. c

Find Out for Yourself

Books

George, Linda. *Plate Tectonics*. California: Kidhaven, 2002.

Meister, Cari. *Volcanoes: Nature's Fury*. Minnesota: ABDO Publishing Company, 1999.

Thompson, Luke. *Volcanoes: Natural Disasters*. New York: Children's Press, 2000.

Web Sites

Use the Internet to find out more about Mauna Loa, volcanoes, and geology with these Web sites.

Volcano World
www.volcanoworld.org
This Web site provides descriptions of many volcanoes. It also answers questions and teaches visitors how to build their own volcano.

Hawai'i Volcanoes National Park
www.nps.gov/havo/home.htm
This Web site offers helpful park information, tells where to view lava safely, and explains the park's history.

Encarta
http://encarta.msn.com
Search this online encyclopedia to find out more about Mauna Loa.

Skill Matching Page

What did you learn? Look at the questions in the "Skills" column. Compare them to the page number of the answers in the "Page" column. Refresh your memory by reading the "Answer" column below.

SKILLS	ANSWER	PAGE
What facts did I learn from this book?	I learned that Mauna Loa means "long mountain" and that it has erupted thirty-nine times since 1832.	5
What skills did I learn?	I learned how to read maps.	5, 16–17
What activities did I do?	I answered the questions in the quiz.	28–29
How can I find out more?	I can read the books and visit the Web sites from the Find Out for Yourself section.	30
How can I get involved?	If I visit the Hawai'i Volcanoes National Park, I will be prepared if an eruption occurs.	22

Glossary

altitudes: heights above sea level
caldera: a giant crater on top of a volcano
cyclonic: associated with tornadoes
endangered: in danger of becoming extinct
evacuation: the act of leaving a location due to danger
extinct: no longer existing
geology: the scientific study of the Earth
lava: melted rock that flows from a volcano
methane gas: a highly flammable, odorless, colorless gas
relocation: moving people to a new home
volcanology: the study and science of volcanoes

Index